WACKY WILD ANIMALS

Brian Moses lives in St. Leonard's-on-Sea with his wife Anne, their two daughters Karen and Linette, two overweight guinea pigs, three nervous fish and a tame squirrel. He spends half his time writing at home and the other half performing his poetry in schools and libraries.

Peter Allen loves his work, drawing. For this book he travelled all over the world, inviting animals back to his house in France to have their pictures done. Luckily they all turned up, except for the bears who were still hibernating and three penguins who had a cold.

Other books in the **TIME FOR A RHYME** series:

MAGNIFICENT MACHINES
poems chosen by John Foster

SPECTACULAR SPOOKS
poems chosen by Brian Moses

FREAKY FAMILIES
poems chosen by David Orme

WACKY WILD ANIMALS

Chosen by Brian Moses

Illustrated by Peter Allen

MACMILLAN CHILDREN'S BOOKS

First published 2000
by Macmillan Children's Books

This edition published 2002 for
The Book People Ltd,
Hall Wood Avenue, Haydock,
St Helens WA11 9UL

ISBN 0 330 39205 0

A CIP catalogue record for this book is available from the British Library

Printed and bound by Mackays of Chatham plc, Kent

Contents

Lion King
Moira Andrew 1

Kangaroos
John Cotton 2

I Wannabe a Wallaby
David Whitehead 4

Big Beast Riddle
Jan Dean 6

Rhino
Gina Douthwaite 8

Animal Riddle
Pie Corbett 9

Bears Don't Like Bananas
John Rice 10

PARTY INVITE from Cyril the Sloth
Patricia Leighton 12

Here Come the Creatures
Wes Magee 14

Giant Anteater
Robin Mellor   16

Camels
Richard Caley   18

A Family Picnic
Dick King-Smith   20

Warthog
Clare Bevan   22

The Crocodile
John Foster   23

Hippopotamus Dancing
Brian Moses   24

Porcupine Valentine
Jane Clarke   26

You Can't Call a Hedgehog Hopscotch
Frances Nagle   27

Penguins on Ice
Celia Warren   28

The Law of the Jungle
Coral Rumble   30

Mole
Tim Pointon   32

Tiger
Mike Jubb   34

The Hippopotamus
Marian Swinger   36

Humming Bird
Jan Dean   37

The Gnat and the Gnu
Paul Bright   38

Pink Flamingos
Andrew Collett   40

A Gorilla in the Night
Andrew Collett   41

Beastly Riddles
Marian Swinger   42

The Itchy Hedgehog
Marian Swinger   45

I Wish I Could Dine With a Porcupine
Brian Moses   46

Monkey Motto
Clare Bevan   48

Pongy Old Musk-Ox
Andrea Shavick   50

Who Am I?
John Kitching   52

Solo Flight
Mike Johnson   54

The Alligator Waiter
Brian Moses   56

Lion King

Topaz stare,
deep as the stone on
Grandad's watch chain.

Bronze coat,
dark as heather honey from
a newly opened pot.

Golden mane,
bright as a king's crown in
the hot yellow sun.

Moira Andrew

Kangaroos

Kangaroos are hoppity
Kangaroos are fun,
If you want to catch a Kangaroo
You'll really have to run.

Kangaroos are jumpy
Bounding over the plain,
You can't hold down a Kangaroo
'Cause he'll bounce up again!

Kangaroos are tough guys
They can box as well,
If a Kangaroo should hit you
Your head rings like a bell!

Kangaroo Mums are kindly
For their young they have a pocket,
Where babies can feed and feel quite safe
While Mum takes off like a rocket!

John Cotton

I Wannabe a Wallaby

I wannabe a wallaby,
A wallaby that's true.
Don't wannabe a possum
A koala or a 'roo.

I wannago hop hopping
Anywhere I please.
Hopping without stopping
Through eucalyptus trees.

A wallaby, a wallaby
Is what I wannabe.
I'd swap my life to be one,
But a problem I can see;

If I'm gonna be a wallaby
I shall have to go and see
If I can find a wallaby,
A very friendly wallaby,
Who would really, really, really . . .

Wannabe . . . ME!

David Whitehead

Big Beast Riddle

What's square and solid
Like a chunky sumo?
Runs like a thunderstorm
Boom, boom boom-o?
Nose like an ice-pick
Sharp and mean-o . . . ?

I know!
I know!
– It's a rhino!

Jan Dean

Rhino

When more than one rhinoceros becomes rhinoceroses, and each of these has horns of hair that stick up from their noses, and armoured skin that wallows in the mud when they reposes, and on each foot each rhino has three hooves instead of toeses - the features of these creatures show the problem language poses when more than one rhino- ceros be - comes rhinoc- eroses.

Gina Douthwaite

Animal Riddle

Like a small **B**ear
　　　　　bundles over the dark road,
　　brushes p**A**st the front gate,
　　　　　as if she owns the joint.
　　Rolls the **D**ustbin,
　　　　　like an expert barrel rider.
Tucks into yesterday's **G**arbage,
　　　　　crunches worms for titbits.
　　Wak**E**s us up from deep sleep,
　　　　　blinks back at torchlight.
　Our midnight feaste**R**,
　　　　　ghost-friend,
　　　　　moon-lit,
　　　　　zebra bear.

Pie Corbett

Bears Don't Like Bananas

Monkeys like to play the drums,
  badgers wear bandannas.
Tigers like to tickle toes
  but bears don't like bananas.

A crocodile can juggle buns
  on visits to his Nana's.
Seagulls like to dance and sing
  but bears don't like bananas.

Rats and mice can somersault
  and do gymnastics with iguanas.
Weasels like to wiggle legs
  but bears don't like bananas.

A porcupine likes drinking tea
  and cheering at gymkhanas.
A ladybird likes eating pies
  but bears don't like bananas.

John Rice

PARTY INVITE from Cyril the Sloth

Having a birthday party
on ahh . . .
      (scratch – yawn – stretch)
Friday next,
that's round about right.
      (scratch – yawn – stretch)

Come as you are
any time you can make it.
      (scratch – yawn – stretch)
I'll be upside down
in my usual spot.
      (scratch – yawn – stretch)

The food's self-service –
fresh leaves and buds.
      (scratch – yawn – stretch)
Grab what you want,
tuck in, don't wait
if I'm having a little nap.

Goodness, I'm tired!
  (yawn – yawn –
      scratch – stretch – curl)
I must have a thousand winks or so,
all this brain work wears a sloth out!

Patricia Leighton

Here Come the Creatures

Here come the Creatures.
One!
Two!
Three!
A crocodile's holding hands with a flea.
A zebra's arm-in-arm with a bee.
A tiger's toddling on with a rat.
An emu's knocking about with a bat.
A warthog's dancing along with a wren.
An elephant's side-by-side with a hen.
Here come the Creatures.
Eight!
Nine!
Ten!

Wes Magee

Giant Anteater

He doesn't eat ice cream
or tall juicy plants,
the Giant Anteater
likes to eat ants!

With his long pointed nose
and his thin sticky tongue,
finding big ants' nests
is his kind of fun.

He can open an ant-hill
with powerful claws,
turning a huge mound
into dust on the floor.

He's not in a hurry.
He has nothing to say.
It's a serious business
eating ants every day.

Robin Mellor

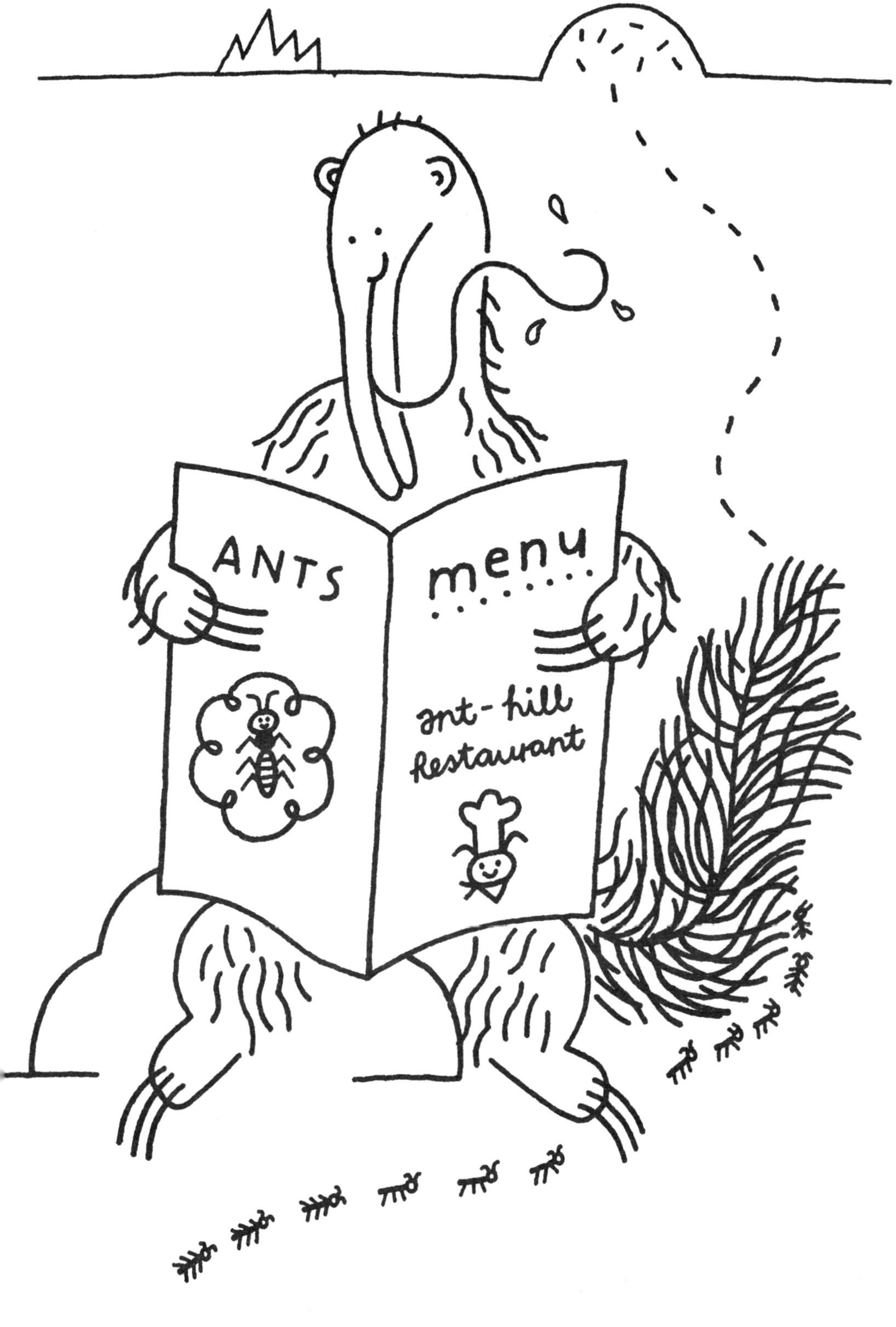
ANTS
menu
ant-hill
Restaurant

Camels

When lions are angry
They roar and roar
When tigers are angry
They strike out a claw
When jackals are angry
They hiss and they jump
But when camels are angry
They just get the hump.

Richard Caley

A Family Picnic

If you meet with a man-eating Tiger,
Don't think that it only eats men.
When it's polished off Dad, it'll start on your mother,
Your sister, your auntie, your new baby brother,
And shortly be hungry again.
For afters, it might manage you and your gran,
So don't think a man-eater only eats man.

Dick King-Smith

Warthog

You say I'm too lumpy
And bumpy and grumpy.
My eyes are too tiny,
My hair is too spiny,
My tusks are too yellow,
My voice is a bellow,
My breath is too smelly,
You laugh at my belly.

I don't need your pity –
My Mum thinks I'm pretty.

Clare Bevan

The Crocodile

The crocodile has a toothy smile.
He opens his jaws with a grin.
He's very polite.
Before taking a bite
He always says, "Please come in!"

John Foster

Hippopotamus Dancing

In the hippo house
at the city zoo,
hippos are moving
to the boogaloo,
big hippos shuffle,
little hippos trot,
everyone giving it
all they've got ...

Hip-hippo, hippopotamus dancing,
hip-hippo, hippopotamus dancing.

Every hippo keeping fit,
fighting the flab
doing their bit,
weight training one week,
aerobics another,
tiny hippopotami
move with their mothers ...

Hip-hippo, hippopotamus dancing,
hip-hippo, hippopotamus dancing.

Hippos in tutus,
hippos in vests,
baby hippos
doing their best
to keep clear of Dad
as he stumbles around,

causing commotion
shaking the ground . . .

Hip-hippo, hippopotamus dancing,
hip-hippo, hippopotamus dancing.

Brian Moses

Porcupine Valentine

Porcupine, oh Porcupine,
Will you be my Valentine?
The touch of your quills sends chills down my spines.
My heart skips a beat whenever we meet.
I love the way you start to rattle
When you stamp your tiny feet.
I adore your sharp claws,
I pine for your spines.
Please be mine,
Porcupine
Valentine.

Jane Clarke

You Can't Call a Hedgehog Hopscotch

You can't call a hedgehog Hopscotch,
It isn't a hedgehog name
And other hedgehogs might mock him.
He'd curl up in shame.

So call him something suitable,
Something a hedgehog would like:
Harry or Prickles or Speedy.
Or, best of all, Spike.

Frances Nagle

Penguins on Ice

Every penguin's mum
can toboggan on her tum.
She can only do that
as she's fluffy and fat:

      It must be nice
      to live on ice.

Every penguin's dad
is happy and glad.
He can slip and slide
and swim and glide:

      It must be nice
      to live on ice.

All penguin chicks
do slippery tricks.
They waddle and fall
but don't mind at all:

      It must be nice
      to live on ice.

Celia Warren

The Law of the Jungle

If you ever meet an elephant
Who tramples on your toes,
Don't let him get away with it –
It's naughtiness, he knows.

If you ever meet a kangaroo
Who bounces on your head,
Don't let him get away with it –
Just send him straight to bed.

And if you ever meet a lion
Who roars into your ear,
Don't let him get away with it –
It's wrong, so make that clear!

Coral Rumble

Mole

A mole is an animal that is rarely found anywhere
  above the ground.
You need to look for a mole

d
o
w
n

a

d
a
r
k

n
a
r
r
o
w

h
o
l
e

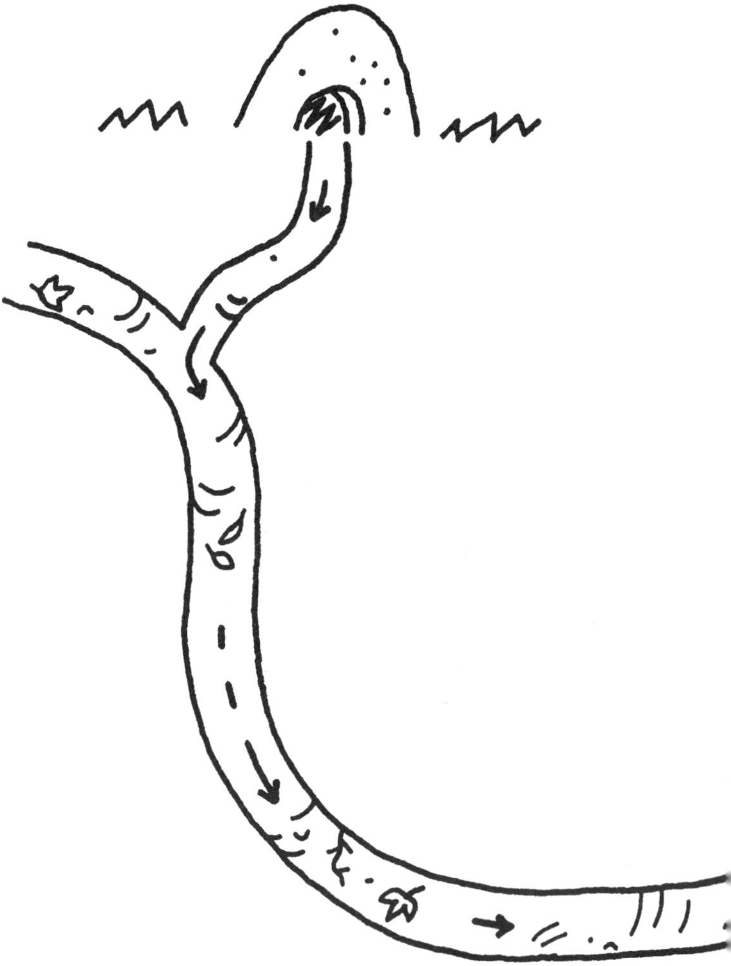

where you'll find him with his big paws and
    twitchy, twitchy nose
building l o n g,   l o n g tunnels where he can
    doze, doze, doze.

Tim Pointon

Tiger

Stripes in the jungle,
Tiger on the prowl;
Creeping through the undergrowth
As quiet as an owl.

Danger in the darkness,
Beware his fearful bite;
And never ever try to stroke
Stripes in the night.

Mike Jubb

The Hippopotamus

The golden sun shines boiling hotamus
down upon the hippopotamus.
It makes her skin come up in spotamus
and gives her sunburn on her bottamus.
So she takes a little trotamus
to where the mud is thick and grottamus,
and sits down with a squelch and splotamus
which cools her skin off quite alotamus.

Marian Swinger

Humming Bird

Humming Bird,   Humming Bird,
    Amazing as   a magic word.
              Rainbows flash out
            From your wings.
             The sweet air
              Through
                your
              feathers
               sings
                 !

Jan Dean

The Gnat and the Gnu

The gnat asked the gnu
As he buzzed round his ear
What's the point of a 'g'
That nobody can hear?

'First answer me this,'
Said the gnu. 'Is it right
You're the one who's been
Buzzing and biting all night?'

'It's my job,' said the gnat,
'And I mean no offence
But back to this "g"
Does it make any sense?'

'In my case,' the gnu said,
'I'd like to suggest
The "g" stands for
Grumpy from getting no rest.'

'In your case . . .' The flick
Of his tail sounded 'Splat!'
'The "g" stands for "Gotcha!"
My thanks for the chat.'

Paul Bright

Pink Flamingos

All flamingos keep a feather duster
underneath their sink
so, before they go to bed each night,
they can tickle each other pink.

Andrew Collett

A Gorilla in the Night

Nothing in the world
could give me such a fright
as seeing a gorilla
in the middle of the night.

One with flashing eyes
and arms to the floor,
growling just outside
my sister's bedroom door.

But nothing in the world
could ever match the treat
of seeing that gorilla
chase my sister down the street.

Andrew Collett

Beastly Riddles

It's big and bad-tempered with horns on its nose.
Don't wake it up if it's having a doze.

rhinoceros

This one has a mane and four velvety paws
and all of the animals run when he roars.

lion

The next one is huge. If you look, you will find
a long trunk in front and a short tail behind.

elephant

There goes a herd and it's moving quite fast
dressed in pyjama stripes, galloping past.

zebra

There's one with patches, long legs and long neck
and a head so high up that it seems like a speck.

giraffe

Who's this in the river, its mouth open wide,
showing rows of sharp teeth? Don't go looking
inside.

crocodile

43

And what's that strange laughing noise?
Creatures are meeting,
slinking around where the lions have been eating.

hyena

And over there, thumping its chest, very strong,
with shining black fur, is a mini King Kong.

gorilla

Marian Swinger

The Itchy Hedgehog

The hedgehog said,
"My prickles make me
very hard to catch
but when a hedgehog itches
it is very hard to scratch."

Marian Swinger

I Wish I Could Dine With a Porcupine

I wish I could dine with a porcupine
or take afternoon tea with a whale.
I wish I could race with a cheetah
or visit the house of a snail.

I wish I could chat with a bat
and learn about its habits.
I wish I could dig a deep burrow
and spend the day with rabbits.

I wish I could fly balloons with baboons
or watch jellyfish eating jelly.
I wish I could perfume spray a skunk
so he wouldn't be quite so smelly.

I wish I could learn about a worm
as I slide along on my tummy,
or meet a baby hippo
and his hippopotamummy.

I wish I could feast with a wildebeest
or rescue a mule from his load.
I wish I could bake a cake with a snake
or hop down the road with a toad.

I wish I could take all these creatures
for a holiday by the sea,
we'd have our own beach barbecue
and toast marshmallows for tea.

Brian Moses

Monkey Motto

I leap through the trees,
I drop to the ground,
That's what I do –
Monkey around.

I pounce on my tail,
I bounce and I bound,
That's what I do –
Monkey around.

I spit out the pips
Of fruit I have found.
That's what I do –
Monkey around.

I hear my own hoots,
I shriek at the sound.
That's what I do –
Monkey around.

Want to have fun
That won't cost a pound?
Here's what you do –
Monkey around.

Clare Bevan

Pongy Old Musk-Ox

The musk-ox grows
A coat to his toes
A coat of musky hair

It gets longer and longer
And pongier and pongier
But it keeps him warm, so who cares?

Andrea Shavick

Who Am I?

My first is in cat but not in dog.
My next is in horse and also in hog.
My third is in ibis but not in goat
My fourth is in monkey, but not found in stoat.
My fifth is in parrot and also in pig.
My sixth is in ant and also earwig.
My next is in newt but not in sow
My eighth is in zebra but never in cow.
My last two in elephant? Twice they appear.
And also you'll find them two times in deer.

Who am I?

John Kitching

Answer: Chimpanzee

Solo Flight

Looks
like a long, long, long way down
to the ground.
Sounds
like a long, long, long way down
to the ground.

Something says
I'm sure to be safe,
because I'm a baby bat,

but,
but,
but I think I'll hang around
for an itsy-bitsy bat-bit longer.

No!
Why mum, why?
time flies
and so must I . . .

Well, if you say so,
first time solo,
here I go.
　　Here I go
　　　Here I go

　　　　　　　　　　I can fly!
　　　　　　　　　I can fly.
　　　　　　　　　I can fly.

Mike Johnson

The Alligator Waiter

Don't give any lip
to an alligator waiter.
Don't growl or howl
when he's on the prowl.
Don't mock him or knock him
or say that he's shocking.
He really isn't
the sort to say:
'Enjoy your meal,'
or, 'Have a nice day!'
And if you should joke
or poke fun at his snout
you'll need to give
your mum a shout.
And make sure you tip
or he'll catch you later.
Don't give any lip
to an alligator waiter.

Brian Moses

slurp!